THE GREAT AMERICAN
BARS AND SALOONS

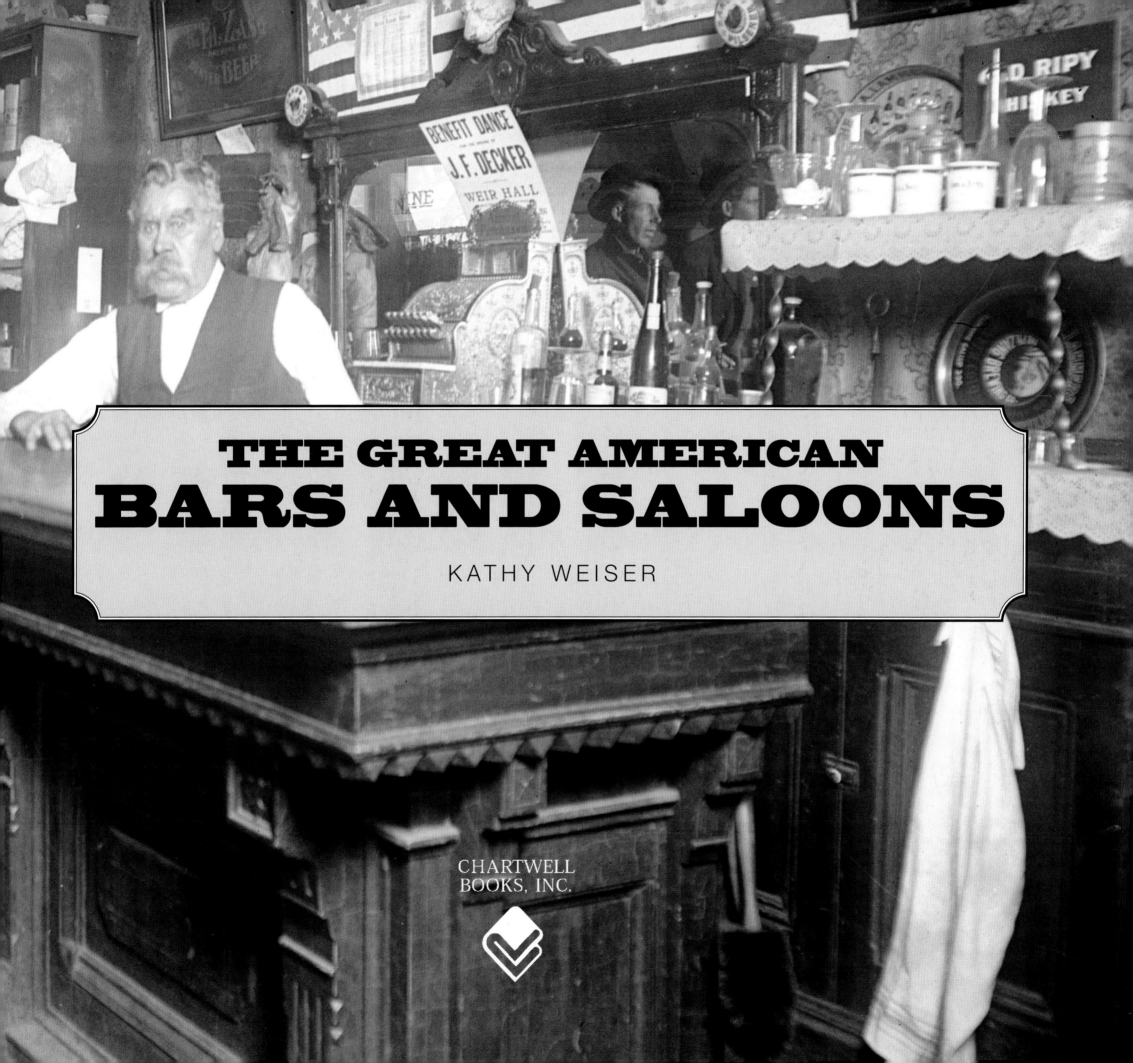

THE GREAT AMERICAN
BARS AND SALOONS

KATHY WEISER

CHARTWELL
BOOKS, INC.

This edition published by
CHARTWELL BOOKS, INC.
A Division of
BOOK SALES, INC.
114 Northfield Avenue
Edison, New Jersey 08837

ISBN-13: 978-0-7858-2138-0
ISBN-10: 0-7858-2138-4

© 2006 by Compendium Publishing Ltd., 43 Frith Street, London W1D 4SA, United Kingdom

Cataloging-in-Publication data is available from the Library of Congress

The Author
A self-described nostalgic soul, Kathy Weiser owns the popular *Legends of America* website (http://legendsofamerica.com), which is filled with facts and fancy about destinations in the American West. She has a business degree, has had a career in corporate management, is now a freelance writer, artist, and photographer, as well as collector of Old West memorabilia and restorer of antiques.

Project Manager: Ray Bonds
Designer: Danny Gillespie
Printed in: China

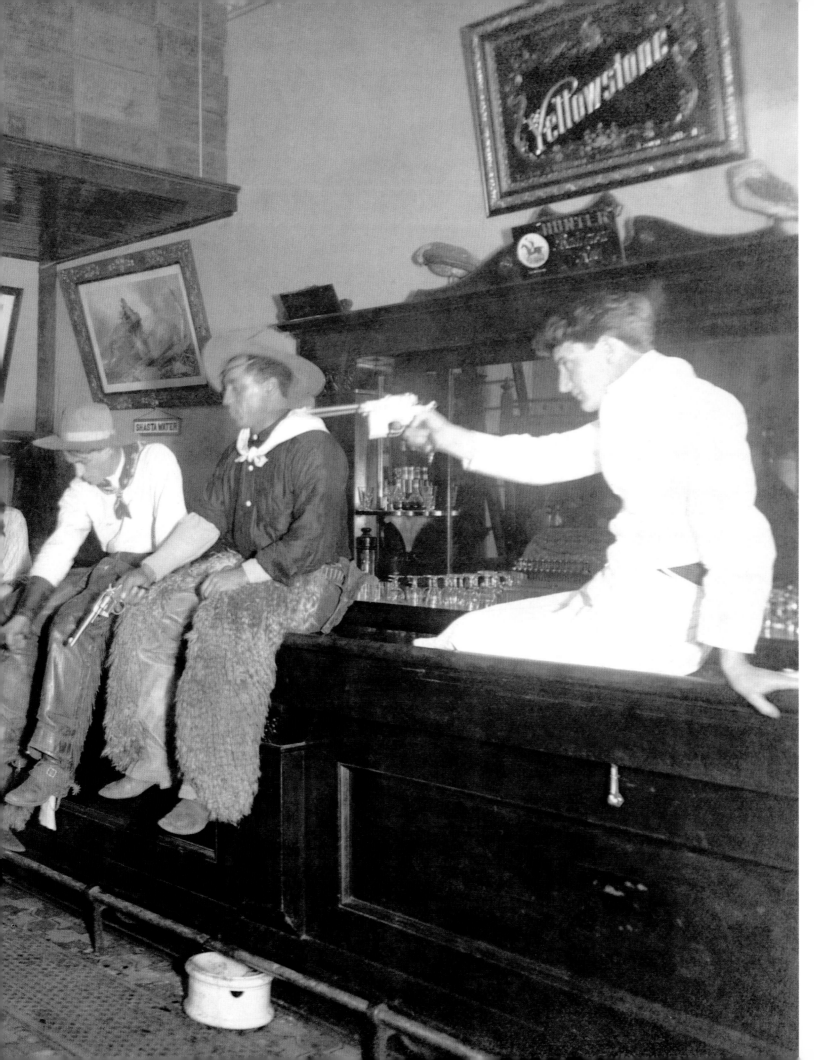

INTRODUCTION

Well, there just ain't no talkin' about the Old West, without mentioning the dozens, no hundreds—even thousands—of saloons of the American West. The very term "saloon" itself, conjures up a picture within our minds of an Old West icon, complete with a wooden false front, a wide boardwalk flanking the dusty street, a couple of hitchin' posts, and the always present swinging doors brushing against the cowboy as he made his way to the long polished bar in search of a whiskey to wet his parched throat.

When America began its movement into the vast West, the saloon was right behind, or more likely, ever present. Though places like Taos and Santa Fe, New Mexico, already held a few Mexican cantinas, they were far and few between until the many saloons of the West began to sprout up wherever the pioneers established a settlement or where trails crossed.

The first place that was actually called a "saloon" was at Brown's Hole near the Wyoming-Colorado-Utah border. Established in 1822, Brown's Saloon catered to the many trappers during the heavy fur trading days.

Saloons were ever popular in a place filled with soldiers, which included one of the West's first saloons at Bent's Fort, Colorado, in the late 1820s; or with cowboys, such as Dodge City, Kansas; and wherever miners scrabbled along rocks or canyons in search of their fortunes. When gold was discovered near Santa Barbara, California, in 1848, the settlement had but one cantina. However, just a few short years later the town boasted more than thirty saloons. In 1883, Livingston, Montana, though it had only 3,000 residents, had thirty-three saloons.

The first Western saloons really didn't fit our classic idea of what a saloon looks like, but rather, were hastily thrown together tents or lean-tos where a lonesome traveler might strike up a conversation, where a cowman might make a deal, or a miner or a soldier might while away their off hours. However, as the settlement became more populated, the saloon would inevitably prosper, taking on the traditional trimmings of the Old West.

In those hard scrabble days, the whiskey served in many of the saloons was some pretty wicked stuff made with raw alcohol, burnt sugar, and a little chewing tobacco. No wonder it took on such names as Tanglefoot, Forty-Rod, Tarantula Juice, Taos Lightning, Red Eye, and Coffin Varnish.

Also popular was Cactus Wine, made from a mix of tequila and peyote tea, and Mule Skinner, made with whiskey and blackberry liquor. The house rotgut was often 100 proof, though it was sometimes cut by the barkeep with turpentine, ammonia, gunpowder or cayenne.

The most popular term for the libation served in saloons was Firewater, which originated when early traders were selling whiskey to the Indians. To convince the Indians of the high alcohol content, the peddlers would pour some of the liquor on the fire, as the Indians watched the fire begin to blaze.

But the majority of Western saloon regulars drank straight liquor—rye or bourbon. If a man ordered a "fancy" cocktail or "sipped" at his drink, he was often ridiculed unless he was "known" or already had a proven reputation as a "tough guy." Unknowns, especially foreigners who often nursed their drinks, were sometimes forced to swallow a fifth of 100 proof at gunpoint "for their own good."

Saloons also served up volumes of beer, but in those days the beer was never ice cold, usually served at 55 to 65 degrees. Though the beer had a head, it wasn't sudsy as it is today. Patrons had to knock back the beer in a hurry before it got too warm or flat. It wasn't until the 1880s that Adolphus Busch introduced artificial refrigeration and pasteurization to the American brewing process, launching Budweiser as a national brand. Before then, folks in the Old West didn't expect their beer to be cold, accustomed as they were to the European

ABOVE LEFT: Three men enjoy a drink in a San Francisco saloon as a peace officer looks on, circa 1900.
Peter Newark's American Pictures

ABOVE: Bartenders and a customer stand at the long bar in what is thought to be Hyman's Saloon in Leadville, Colorado, circa 1883-1889. It was here that the last man to be shot by Doc Holliday was wounded, in August 1884. As Billy Allen, a former adversary from Tombstone, entered the bar, Holliday fired on him, hitting him in the arm. Surprisingly, on March 28, 1885, a jury found Holliday not guilty of the shooting or attempted murder.
Denver Public Library

tradition of beer served at room temperature.

In virtually every mining camp and prairie town a poker table could be found in each saloon, surrounded by prospectors, lawmen, cowboys, railroad workers, soldiers, and outlaws waiting for a chance to tempt fortune and fate. Faro was by far the most popular and prolific game played in Old West saloons, followed by brag, three-card-monte, and dice games such as high-low, chuck-a-luck and grand hazard. Before long many of the Old West mining camps such as Deadwood, Leadville, and Tombstone became as well known for gunfights over card games as they did for their wealth of gold and silver ore. Professional gamblers such as Doc Holliday and Wild Bill Hickok learned early to hone their six-shooter skills at the same pace as their gambling abilities. Taking swift action upon the green cloth became part of the gamblers' code—shoot first and ask questions later.

Eventually, there was every type of saloon that one could imagine. There were gambling saloons, restaurant saloons, billiard saloons, dance hall saloons, bowling saloons, and, of course, the ever present, plain ole' fashioned, "just drinking" saloons. They took on names such as the First Chance Saloon in Miles City, Montana, the Bull's Head in Abilene, Kansas, and the Holy Moses in Creede, Colorado. In many of the more populated settlements, these saloons never closed, catering to their ever present patrons twenty-four hours a day, seven days a week. Some didn't even bother to have a front door that would close.

In almost every saloon, one could depend on seeing the long paneled bar, usually made of oak or mahogany, and polished to a splendid shine. Encircling the base of the bar would be a gleaming brass foot rail with a row of spittoons spaced along the floor next to the bar. Along the ledge, the saloon patrons would find towels hanging so that they might wipe the beer suds from their mustaches.

Decorations at these many saloons varied from place to place but most often reflected the ideals of the customers. In the cowtowns of the prairies, one might see steer horns, spurs, and saddles adorning the walls, while in the mountains, a customer would be met by the glazing eyes of taxidermied deer or elk. Often, there was the infamous painting of a nude woman hanging behind the bar.

The regulars at saloons often acquired calluses on their elbows by prolonged and heavy leaning on the bar. Men of the West usually did not drink alone nor did they drink at home and, needing each other's company, there were a lot of regulars at the many saloons. The patrons were a varied lot—from miners to outlaws, to gamblers and honest workmen. What they were not were minorities. Saloons of the West did not welcome other races. Indians were excluded by law. An occasional black man might be grudgingly accepted, or at least ignored, if he happened to be a noted gambler or outlaw. If a Chinese man entered a saloon, he risked his life.

However, there was one type of "white man" that was also generally not welcome. That was the soldier. There were several reasons for this. Given the makeup of the many men of the West—adventurers, people who "didn't fit in" in the East, outlaws, and Civil War deserters—they had no respect for the men who "policed the West." Nor could these independent-minded men respect anyone who was made to "stand at attention" and obey all orders. Finally, for some unknown reason, they blamed the soldier for infecting the parlor house girls with diseases. Due to the culture at the time, also excluded were "respectable" women. Unless they were a saloon girl or a "shady lady," women did not enter saloons, a tradition that lasted until World War I. In retaliation, the ladies were primarily behind the Prohibition movement.

These private men of the West were also accustomed to inquiring of another man's first name only. With their varied and often shady backgrounds, curiosity was considered impolite. Both men's and women's pasts were respected and were not inquired about. To break this unwritten rule could be very unhealthy for the inquirer, who might end up dead

LEFT: Owned by the Dodge City sheriff, Ham Bell's Variety Saloon was the first saloon where the infamous can-can dance was performed. Note that this is one of only a few photographs that actually show women inside a saloon. Circa early 1900s.
Peter Newark's American Pictures

OVERLEAF LEFT: Though soldiers were not always welcomed in many of the saloons of the West, this was not the case in Fort Keogh, Montana, in the early 1890s.
Corbis

OVERLEAF RIGHT: Skramstad's Liquor Store and Saloon takes pride of position in the left foreground of this 1908 photo of the main business street in Goodhue, Minnesota, looking north. Minnesota, whose name derives from the Indian name for Minnesota River (*mini sota*, which means smoky-white or sky-tinted water), became the 32nd state when it joined the United States in 1858. Minnesota is referred to as The Land of 10,000 Lakes," although it actually has more than 15,000.

in the street in front of the saloon. For instance, one would never ask a rancher the size of his herd, which would be tantamount to asking a man to see his income tax return today.

Another custom was the expected offer to treat the man standing next to you to a drink. If a stranger arrived and didn't make the offer, he would often be asked why he hadn't done so. Even worse was refusing a drink, which was considered a terrible insult, regardless of the vile liquor that might be served. On one such occasion at a Tucson, Arizona, saloon, a man who refused the offer was taken from bar to bar at gunpoint until "he learned some manners." However, if a man came in and confessed that he was broke and needed a drink,

few men would refuse him. On the other hand, if he ordered a drink, knowing that he couldn't pay for it, he might find himself beaten up or worse.

Because the saloon was usually one of the first and bigger buildings within many new settlements, it was common that it was also utilized as a public meeting place. Judge Roy Bean and his combination saloon and courtroom in Langtry, Texas, was a prime example of this practice. Another saloon in Downieville, California, was not only the most popular saloon in town, but also the office of the local Justice of the Peace. In Hays City, Kansas, the first church services were held in Tommy Drum's Saloon.

9. MAIN BUSINESS ST. LOOKING NORTH.

Several noted gunmen of the West owned saloons, tended bar or dealt cards at one time or another. These included such famous characters as Wild Bill Hickok, Bill Tighman, Ben Daniels, Wyatt Earp, Bat Masterson, Ben Thompson, Doc Holliday, and many others. But, most notable among the many saloons of the West was the ever present violence that was instigated or occurred within these establishments. In 1876, Bob Younger said, "We are rough men and used to rough ways." Couple that with the public access, flow of potent whiskey, and the general lawlessness of the times, and the saloon was an inevitable powder keg.

There were numerous killings inside of these Old West saloons. Wild Bill Hickok, for example, was killed by Jack McCall while playing poker in the No. 10 Saloon in Deadwood, South Dakota; Bob Ford, Jesse James's killer, was shot down in his own tent saloon in Creede, Colorado; and John Wesley Hardin was shot and killed from behind on August 19, 1895, in an El Paso, Texas, saloon. Many other acts of violence were instigated in saloons, which wound up with shoot-outs in the street, or public hangings after vigilante groups had formed within a saloon.

And we must not forget the saloon or dance hall girl, whose job was to brighten the

ABOVE: **As a stranger pulls into Ehrenburg, Arizona Territory, on his pioneer cross-country automobile tour, townspeople surround the "new-fangled" Model-T, as a wagon and two saloons sit in the background. Photo by A. L. Westgard, circa 1911.**
Corbis

evenings of lonely men starved of female companionship. Contrary to what many might think, the saloon girl was very rarely a prostitute—this tended to occur only in the very shabbiest class of saloons. Although the "respectable" ladies considered the saloon girls "fallen," most of the girls wouldn't be caught dead associating with an actual prostitute. Their job was to entertain the guests, sing for them, dance with them, talk to them, and perhaps flirt with them a little—inducing them to remain in the bar, buying drinks and patronizing the games.

Not all saloons employed saloon girls. Dodge City's north side of Front Street, for example, was the "respectable" side, where guns, saloon girls, and gambling were barred. Instead, music and billiards were featured as the chief amusements to accompany drinking.

Most saloon girls were refugees from farms or mills, lured by posters and handbills advertising high wages, easy work, and fine clothing. Many were widows or other needy women of good morals, forced to earn a living in an era that offered few means for women to do so. Earning as much as $10 per week, most saloon girls also made a commission from the drinks that they sold. Whiskey sold to the customer was marked up thirty to sixty percent over its wholesale price. Commonly, drinks bought for the girls would only be cold tea or colored sugar water served in a shot glass; however, the customer was charged the full price of whiskey, which could range from ten to seventy-five cents a shot.

In most places the proprieties of treating the saloon girls as ladies were strictly observed, as much because Western men tended to revere all women as because the women or the saloon keeper demanded it. Any man who mistreated these women would quickly become a social outcast, and if he insulted one he would very likely be killed.

While they might have been scorned by the "proper" ladies, the saloon girls could count on respect from the males. And as for the "respectable women," the saloon girls were rarely interested in the opinions of the drab, hard-working women who set themselves up to judge them. In fact, they were hard pressed to understand why those women didn't have sense enough to avoid working themselves to death by having babies, tending animals, and helping their husbands try to bring in a crop or tend the cattle. However, even today, don't we still see the vestige remains of the Old West saloon as the professional woman may peer down upon the bar waitress, who in turn may peer down upon today's prostitute?

In the early California Gold Rush of 1849, dance halls began to appear and spread throughout the boomtowns. While these saloons usually offered games of chance, their chief attraction was dancing. The customer generally paid 75¢ to $1.00 for a ticket to dance, with the proceeds being split between the dance hall girl and the saloon owner. After the dance, the girl would steer the gentleman to the bar, where she would make an additional commission from the sale of a drink.

As the years moved forward into the 20th century, the days of the Old West were winding down. Railroads replaced stagecoaches, the growth of cities was bringing culture to the West, most of the notorious outlaws were dead or in jail, and Wyatt Earp had settled down to tell his frontier tales to any and every book author and silent movie producer in Hollywood. Meanwhile, as the savage West was slowly being tamed, a new movement had been emerging in the East, to curb or stop the consumption of alcohol. Often associated with poverty, crime, corruption, social problems, and increasing taxes, alcohol was considered the source of all evil by those behind the Temperance and Prohibition movements. Saloons were accused of being dens of iniquity by those behind these movements, a fact that was most often true.

Having started in the 1830s, temperance advocates didn't initially support prohibiting consumption of alcohol, but rather, the drinking of beer and wine in moderation and abstention from hard liquor. By 1855, thirteen of the then thirty-one, states had passed laws prohibiting the manufacture and sale of intoxicating liquors. However, the momentum came

to a screeching halt during the Civil War, and afterwards the hardened soldiers returning from the war wanted nothing to do with temperance, and it was given little attention for the next two decades.

However, as more and more women entered the vast West, "proper" women began to see saloons as hotbeds of vice, where not only drinking was encouraged, but also gambling, prostitution, dancing, and tobacco use. Becoming politically active for the first time, these many women joined the fight in the 1880s and the cause was reborn. By the turn of the century, Carrie Nation was taking an ax to saloons, and members of the Anti-Saloon League and the Women's Christian Temperance Union were marching in the streets, halting traffic with their demands that saloons close their doors. No longer satisfied with accepting the use of alcohol in moderation, these advocates now demanded total prohibition. Within a few short years the "frenzy" of these groups grew to include a political movement where large numbers of voters demanded that government lead the country in a strong stand of moral leadership.

In 1917, the 18th Amendment to the Constitution, which prohibited the "manufacture, sale, or transportation of intoxicating liquors," was drafted and passed into national legislation the following year. Called the "noble experiment" by Herbert Hoover, seventy-five percent of the states ratified the Amendment the next year. In 1920, the Volstead Act was passed to enforce the amendment.

Prohibition advocates initially rejoiced in their "successes," as arrests for drunkenness declined and medical statistics showed a marked decrease in treatments for alcohol-related illnesses. Statistics also demonstrated that drinking in general decreased. However, the decline had been the trend for several years before Prohibition, and many felt that any further decrease was due to the high cost of bootlegged liquor, rather than the law itself. For a time, Prohibition maintained some of its success, especially in rural areas, though liquor continued to flow with relative ease in the cities.

However, with the end of World War I and the nation in high spirits, the demand for liquor quickly increased and another culture emerged for those who saw opportunity and financial gain in thwarting the new law and fulfilling the public demand. Bootleggers, illegal

alcohol traffickers, and speakeasies began to multiply by the hundreds. Though they may have appeared to close down for a short period, saloons simply went "underground" in basements, attics, upper floors, and disguised as other businesses, such as cafes, soda shops, and entertainment venues. Given the name because of the need to whisper or "speak easy," these many illegal drinking enterprises quickly became established institutions, so much so that some said that, for every former legitimate saloon that closed, it was replaced by a half-dozen illegal "gin joints." At one time, there were thought to be over 100,000 speakeasies in New York City alone; New Jersey claimed there were ten times as many as before the Amendment; and Rochester, New York, twice the number. The same became true all over the nation.

Gone were the boardwalks, swinging doors, spittoons, and mustache towels of the saloon era, but hiding behind a number of "false fronts" were thousands of illegal speakeasies. Generally, before a thirsty patron could cross the illegal threshold, a password, specific handshake or secret knock was required. Gone also were the tinkling sounds of the piano player and dance hall girls, as Prohibition ushered in the age of jazz. Having been long banned from the saloons of the past, "regular" women found easy entrance into these new establishments. Prior to the Amendment, women drank very little, and even then perhaps just a drop of wine or sherry. But, just six months after Prohibition became law in 1920, women got the right to vote and, coming into their own, they quickly "loosened" up, tossed their corsets, and enjoyed their newfound freedoms.

The "Jazz Age" quickly signified a loosening up of morals, the exact opposite of what the Prohibition advocates had intended, and in came the "flappers." With short skirts and bobbed hair, they flooded the speakeasies, daring to smoke cigarettes and drink cocktails. Dancing to the tunes of such soon-to-be famous jazz greats as Louis Armstrong, Duke Ellington, Bojangles Robinson, and Ethel Waters, their powdered faces, bright red lips, and bare arms and legs displayed an abandon never before seen by American women. Quickly, both Prohibition and jazz music were blamed for the immorality of women, as well as young people who were attracted to the glamor of speakeasies.

No longer did the free-flowing liquor in speakeasies carry its former names of White

Lightning, Tanglefoot, and Firewater; alcohol now carried the new monikers of cocktail, devil's candy, bathtub gin, booze, and hooch. Where beer and wine had previously been the drinks of choice, now strong alcohol was drunk much more frequently, since it was easier to transport and took up less space, making it cheaper for speakeasy patrons. It was at this time that the "cocktail" was born, which had virtually been non-existent prior to Prohibition. In the days of the "Old West," most men drank either beer or straight shots of liquor. However, during this new era that welcomed women, alcohol began to be mixed with soft drinks, sugar-water, and fruit juices. With the bootlegged liquor being much more palatable, millions of people who didn't like the taste of beer, wine, or hard liquors found cocktails irresistible, turning men and women alike into "criminals" by the thousands.

While often having their cocktails in teacups, in case of a raid, old social barriers were broken, as the rich and powerful began to rub shoulders with ordinary folks. From housewives to large business owners, blue collar workers, corrupted police chiefs and mayors, these many patrons befriended each other in their quest of the same goals—drinking and avoiding the law prohibiting it.

Like their counterpart saloons of the past, prostitution and gambling flourished in speakeasies. But they also introduced a new element to their patrons—drugs. Many who would never have come into contact with these substances found a new source of "entertainment" in the permissive atmosphere of the speakeasies. Narcotics, hashish, and marijuana were soon used in abundance.

To supply these many illegal establishments with beer, wine, and liquor, organization was required, hence the birth of organized crime. Into this crime-ripe environment walked such characters as Al "Scarface" Capone in Chicago, the Purple Gang of Detroit, Lucky Luciano in New York, and hundreds of others. The large majority of speakeasies were established and controlled by organized criminals, who opened everything from plush nightclubs to dark and smoky basement taverns. Though raids became a daily federal pastime, law enforcement agencies couldn't keep up with the spread of alcohol consumption and establishments. When the enforcers were successful in targeting a "gin joint," the club owners, anticipating a raid, were often able to disguise the true intent of their businesses, with

ABOVE LEFT: The growing antipathy toward alcohol and drinking establishments is epitomized in this photo, by J. M. Naiman, of The Anti-Saloon League at Washington, D.C., December 8, 1921.
Library of Congress

ABOVE: Rather than reducing consumption of alcohol, Prohibition actually increased it, especially among those not known to have drunk before. Here a woman hides a liquor flask in her boot on January 21, 1922.
Library of Congress

ABOVE: **Booze on the run! Prohibition officers in Zion City, Illinois, proudly display bottles of beer that were part of a consignment of truckloads of bootleg alcohol on their way to Chicago (c1910-1920). This is one lot that didn't get to the speakeasies.**
Library of Congress

ABOVE: Drinking and open gambling went side
by side in this crowded bar in Reno, Nevada,
seen in October 1908. Casino gambling wasn't
legalized in Nevada until 1931.
Library of Congress

ABOVE: **Though thousands of barrels of beer and liquor were confiscated by federal officers, they couldn't keep up with the liquor traffickers, circa 1921-1932.**
Library of Congress

ABOVE RIGHT: **Men pose in a warehouse filled with confiscated liquor during Prohibition, circa 1921-1932.**
Library of Congress

elaborate alarms installed and their illegal contraband hidden in drop-shelves and secret cabinets. Other establishments didn't even bother with hiding or disguising the liquor, as they paid out part of their profits to Prohibition agents and police officers, leading to a monumental amount of political corruption.

Increasingly, organized crime groups controlled the liquor industry, which led to turf wars and gang murders, the worst of which was the St. Valentine's Day Massacre of 1929 in Chicago. Seven men were killed in this incident during the increasingly violent war over liquor control, with the blame put at Capone's door. Though gaining the most attention, this was just one violent event of the era; by the late 1920s, Chicago authorities reported as many as 400 gangland murders each year. And Chicago was not alone in its high crime rate, as virtually every city across the nation was rife with illegal liquor trafficking, speakeasies, and the violence that they bred.

As the newspapers across the country screamed horrific headlines, the public increasingly blamed Prohibition for the violence, as well as the political corruption that had become rampant throughout the Nation. While the solution was placed within the jurisdiction of the Treasury Department for enforcement, the department's untrained Prohibition officers faced huge challenges in budget constraints and with little support from the public. Before long, groups began to organize to repeal Prohibition, especially after the Great Depression, when people were looking for jobs, ones that could be created if breweries,

distilleries, and taverns could reopen. Even Herbert Hoover was forced to admit that the 18th Amendment was offering more harm than good.

By 1932, both presidential candidates, Franklin D. Roosevelt and Herbert Hoover, favored repeal. When elected, Roosevelt backed the repeal and on December 5, 1933, the Twenty-first Amendment to the Constitution officially repealed the Eighteenth Amendment, and the "Noble Experiment" came to an end.

When Prohibition finally ended, the word "saloon" had virtually disappeared from American vocabulary, and legal drinking establishments once again opened in abundance, referring to themselves as "cocktail lounges" and "taverns."

Today, we still see the remains of both the "Old West" saloon and the jazz-age speakeasy in popular bars across the country. Although the spittoons, pistols, flappers, and flasks are long gone, these many establishments remain a place where business people continue to make deals, men and women socialize, and patrons frequent to chase away their cares. Whether it's called a saloon, a speakeasy, a bar, or a tavern, these recession-proof businesses will no doubt live not only in our rich history, but long into our future.

ABOVE: Law enforcement officers pour
bottles of confiscated liquor into the sewer
in the late 1920s.
Library of Congress

RIGHT: Though women were a major force in
leading the nation towards the passage of the
18th Amendment, they were also instrumental
in repealing the law that had failed to meet its
objectives. In this photo, taken about 1933, they
celebrate the end of Prohibition, by toasting a
beer in a frosty mug.
Bettman/Corbis

LEFT: Written on the back of this early 1900s photograph are the words, "Sins of the Father," aptly expressing America's sentiment at the time. Undaunted, this beefy bartender pours a beer for an unseen thirsty patron.
Bettman/Corbis

ABOVE: McSorley's Old Ale House in East 7th Street, NYC, established in 1854 and laying claim to being the oldest tavern in the city, still offers no-frills light or dark ale, and did not allow females in until 1970 (when the "Good Ale, Raw Onions, and No Ladies" philosophy still prevailed). With sawdust on the floor, ceiling-hung fans, exposed stove and heating pipes, the Irish atmosphere is boisterous and, well, "beery"—none more so than on St. Patrick's Day. Patrons have never seemed to mind having to line up for an hour or so to get in.
JP Laffont/Sygma/Corbi

HISTORIC BARS AND SALOONS ACROSS THE NATION

RIGHT: Fraunces Tavern, at the corner of Board and Pearl Streets, is said to be the oldest structure in Manhattan, NYC. The building was purchased by ambitious innkeeper Samuel Fraunces in 1762, and was originally called the "Queen's Head," after Queen Charlotte, wife of the English King George III. Fraunces ran the establishment as a restaurant, and it was patronized by many important figures of the Revolution, none more so than George Washington. It was here that Washington bade his emotional farewell to his Continental Army officers before retiring to Mount Vernon in 1783.
Bettmann/Corbis

ABOVE: In 1873 there were fifteen saloons in Wichita, and Fritz Snitzler's Saloon and Restaurant was one of the most popular. The establishment not only provided a setting for eating and drinking, but also games of chance and dancehall girls. In this historic photograph, several "girls" can be seen on the rooftop above Snitzler's sign.
Peter Newark's American Pictures

RIGHT: The Erin Go Bragh Saloon in Duluth, Minnesota, photographed by B. F. Childs in about 1875, displays the typical trappings of boardwalk and false fronts so often associated with saloons of the past. However, unlike so many of its Western counterparts, instead of a dusty street, St. Louis Avenue provides a murky swamp.
Minnesota Historical Society/Corbis

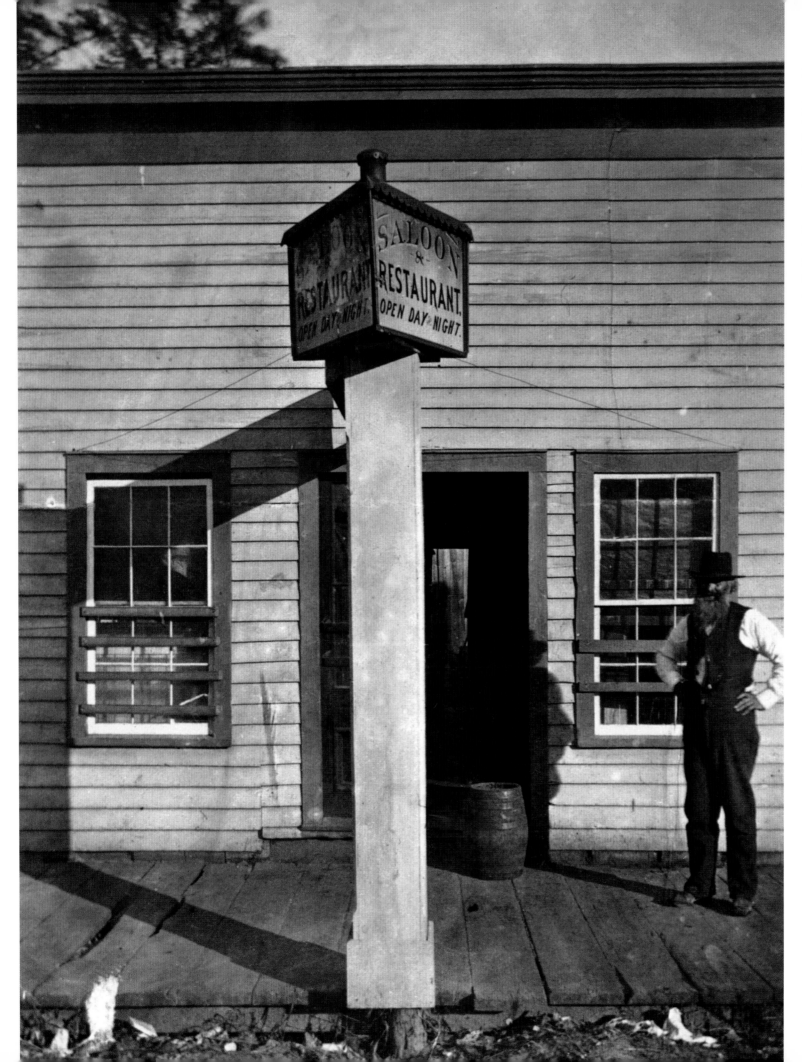

FAR LEFT: **Chan Gow, one of several Chinese men in Georgetown, Colorado, sits next to a pitbull in a two-wheel cart pulled by a burro. Behind him, several men and boys stand before a saloon, which advertises Coors Golden Beer and pure rye whiskey, circa 1875-1892.**
Denver Public Library

LEFT: **A bearded old man and a tall sign welcome customers to the Brainerd Saloon and Restaurant in Brainerd, Minnesota, in about 1881.**
Minnesota Historical Society/Corbis

LEFT: Five men and the saloonkeeper stand before the Old Red Front Saloon in La Junta, Colorado, in 1882, the top of the storefront windows sporting the sign "Inebreates Home."
Denver Public Library

ABOVE: **The Original Blue Front Saloon in La Junta, Colorado, seen in about 1883, displays the new name of Zang's Beer across the top of its false front. An aproned bartender stands before its double doors, welcoming customers in for a drink.**
Denver Public Library

OVERLEAF LEFT: **The Long Branch Saloon in Dodge City, Kansas, was a popular haunt of Wyatt Earp and Doc Holliday. Though located north of Dodge City's "Deadline," which prohibited gambling, Doc Holliday was known to have dealt cards in a back room of the saloon.**
Peter Newark's American Pictures

OVERLEAF RIGHT: **This old-fashioned saloon in Socorro, New Mexico, shown in the 1880s, displays the typical wall décor seen in many of these popular drinking establishments of the time, including pictures of women, mirrors, and liquor advertising upon its walls.**
Peter Newark's American Pictures

LEFT: **With the coming of the railroad in the 1880s, miners, merchants, and cattlemen arrived in large numbers to the small community of Socorro, New Mexico. With rich silver deposits found in the Socorro Peak District, the settlement became a boomtown sporting a number of saloons, including Wilton's, pictured here with a number of men relaxing outside, circa 1887.**
Peter Newark's American Pictures

ABOVE: **Women peer from the balcony of George Fechter's Farmer's Home Saloon, Hotel and Restaurant in Moorhead, Minnesota, in the 1880s. Though some might wonder if these women were actually "painted ladies," often portrayed in Western films as enticing customers from the balconies of brothels, it is unlikely that these women held that dubious distinction. Tightly regulated, Moorhead segregated its "red light district" to another part of the city.**
Clay County, Minnesota Historical Society

RIGHT: William "Billy" Reese, seated inside the doorway of his saloon in the 1880s, poses with several men, a young girl, a dog, and a cat, in front of his business. Atop his saloon in Pitkin, the sign proudly displays that he is an agent for Anheuser Busch St. Louis Beer. Pitkin, originally named Quartzville, was Colorado's first mining camp west of the Continental Divide.
Denver Public Library

FAR RIGHT: Inside Reese's Saloon, Billy serves a drink to Jack and Pete Stroller as they stand at the end of the mirror-backed bar. The saloon's interior displays the typical décor of most Old West bars; however, it also includes a billiards table, not so common in those times.
Denver Public Library

LEFT: **Saloons of the West often reflected their surroundings and such was the case in this one in Leadville, Colorado, shown between 1880 and 1910. The walls are filled with the taxidermied heads of deer, elk, sheep, and mountain goats. Also pictured with the customers are several gaming machines and an old time music box that instructs, "Drop Nickle in Top Right Hand Side, Pull Lever."**
Denver Public Library

RIGHT: **Yet another mining camp in Colorado (shown between 1880 and 1910), Georgetown sported its share of saloons, including this one which advertises "Coors Golden Beer" and "Wines and Liquors" for its patrons. Lounging on the typical long boardwalk before the dusty street are the proprietor and two customers.**
Denver Public Library

ABOVE: In a business building between Platte and Central in Denver, Colorado, are the Depot Rooming House, Depot Restaurant, and the Beer Depot, seen in the 1880s. Along the side of the building is an advertisement for the Union Brewery located several blocks away.
Denver Public Library

OVERLEAF LEFT: Several men pose in front of the Headquarters Saloon in Wilcox, Arizona, in the 1880s. It was here that Warren Earp, the youngest of the fabled Earp brothers, met his demise. A bartender at the saloon, Warren was killed during a drunken argument on July 6, 1900.
Peter Newark's American Pictures

OVERLEAF RIGHT: In Sonora, Texas, one of the last frontier towns of the Lone Star state, the Favorite Saloon is filled with a number of thirsty cowboys (1890s).
Peter Newark's American Pictures

ABOVE: **Cowboys lounge at the rail of a popular Tascosa, Texas, saloon in the 1890s. A thriving cow town in the Texas Panhandle, the town died when one of the major railroads bypassed the settlement. It soon became a ghost town and is now part of Cal Farley's Boys Ranch.**
Peter Newark's American Pictures

RIGHT: **In the 1890s, it was not unusual for a barbershop to be located next door to a saloon or, in the case of this tent saloon in the Southwest, operating right inside.**
Peter Newark's American Pictures

LEFT: The bartender stands ready for custom, or trouble, with his handgun in a glass next to him, in an Albany County, Wyoming saloon, circa 1890s.
Peter Newark's American Pictures

ABOVE: Located at the crossroads of the Oregon Trail and routes to the Boise Basin and Owyhee mining districts, Boise, Idaho, thrived as a prosperous commercial center in the late 19th century. As with other Old West settlements, Boise's prosperity brought a number of saloons, including M. C. Smith's, pictured here in about 1890 with a number of men standing out front.
Idaho State Historical Society

LEFT: Hanson & Peterson's Gold Mine Saloon was just one of many that thrived during the 1890s in Moorhead, Minnesota. *Clay County, Minnesota Historical Society*

LEFT: Judge Roy Bean, self-described as the "Law West of the Pecos," holds court upon the boardwalk porch of his saloon and "Hall of Justice," in Langtry, Texas, about 1900. Here, Bean is trying a horse-thief. Left of the judge is the stolen horse, as well as two accomplice horse-thieves, guarded by an officer.
Peter Newark's American Pictures

ABOVE: **Judge Roy Bean (bearded) stands before his popular Jersey Lilly Saloon in Langtry, Texas, in 1893. Named for Lillie Langtry, a British actress that Bean had never met but was infatuated with, the saloon not only served up volumes of beer and whiskey, it also served as his personal court room. Here, he sentenced dozens of men to the gallows and soon earned the nickname "Hanging Judge Roy Bean." Today, the saloon still stands as a museum in the dusty streets of Langtry.** *Corbis*

RIGHT: **Hanson & Peterson's Gold Mine Saloon was just one of many that thrived during the 1890s in Moorhead, Minnesota.** *Clay County, Minnesota Historical Society*

LEFT: **Thirsty men gather around a shipment of kegs to "The Bijou" Saloon in Round Pond, Oklahoma. Photo by Kennett, circa January, 1894.**
National Archives

ABOVE: **At 12:00 noon on September 16, 1893, more than 100,000 men, women and children lined up to race for 40,000 land claims in the Cherokee Outland Land Run. By nightfall, a city of canvas, with a population of over 40,000 people, had settled in what became known as "Hell's Half-Acre." The makeshift town soon included a number of businesses, including the ever-present saloons. Later, the overnight camp would become the town of Perry, Oklahoma.**
Corbis

ABOVE: In one of many towns born of the Oklahoma Land Runs, Round Pond shopkeepers and customers pose in the doorways of Broadway Street, including those of the **Wilson Saloon (far left) and the Nelson Restaurant. Photo by Kennett, circa January, 1894.** *Corbis*

RIGHT: Prospectors stand in front of the Jeff Smith Parlor in Skagway, Yukon Territory, Canada, in the 1890s. The saloon was owned by the notorious conman, Jefferson "Soapy" Smith, who followed the Klondike Gold Rush to Skagway after having bilked hundreds of men and women in Colorado. Initially, Smith was popular in the mining camp, until the townfolk began to catch on to his many schemes. He was killed in a duel on the waterfront. *PEMCO-Webster & Stevens Collection; Museum of History and Industry, Seattle/Corbis*

RIGHT: **Typically in mining camps, many saloons began as little more than a tent. This is true of these tent businesses of Gurrys Business Block in Deering, Alaska, during the Klondike Gold Rush, circa 1903. The tents include four stores and a combination baker and saloon.**
Bettman/Corbis

The Comerco Saloon Nome, Alaska

LEFT: Popular during the Klondike Gold Rush, the Commerce Saloon in Nome, Alaska, displays the typical trappings of the Old West saloon, including the long polished bar, the brass hand and foot rails, mustache towels, and spittoons.
Bettman/Corbis

ABOVE: Though the long bar remains spit-and-polished, the proprietors of this busy saloon, during the Gold Rush days in Dawson, Alaska, don't bother with the floor that sees a wealth of daily traffic.
Bettman/Corbis

FAR LEFT: This street scene in Rawhide, Nevada, is extremely typical of many of the settlements in the vast West during the early years of the 20th century. Bustling with wagons, horses, cowhands, and miners, Rawhide boomed in 1906 when gold was discovered, only to quickly die when the ore played out. Today, all that's left of Rawhide is the old stone jail and two water towers. Photo by McClelland.
Corbis

LEFT: Frontier hardscrabble and resilient pioneers, including a girl and a small child, stand before a railroad terminus in 1895.
Bettman/Corbis

THIS IS THE
GOLORADO LIQUOR HOUSE

LUCK TAFT &
COUNTRYMAN.

MINING ENGINEERS.

NEVER CLOSED.

HOT FREE LUNCH
DAY & NIGHT.

WINE
ROOMS IN
CONNECTION

HOT FREE LUNCH
DAY & NIGHT.

COORS EXTRA BREW.

COORS EXTRA BREW.

THE
COLORADO
LIQUOR HOUSE.

COLORADO
LIQUOR HOUSE.

THE COLORADO LIQUOR
HOUSE.

LEFT: **During the 1890s, bowler-hat-adorned Chuck Connors acted as an urban tour guide to visitors and locals wanting to see the seedy and exotic side of Chinatown in New York City. Visiting opium dens, complete with slave girls, and witnessing brutal knife fights, the tourists were unaware that the sights were staged by Connors and his friends. Wildly popular, Connors became known as the "Mayor of Chinatown."**
Bettman/Corbis

ABOVE: **The Colorado Liquor House in Cripple Creek served hundreds of miners in its spacious two-story building located at the corner of Myers Avenue and 3rd Street. Myers Avenue was known as one of the liveliest streets in the Old West, with the phrase, "There'll be a Hot Time in the Old Town Tonight" coined after it. Filled with parlor houses, "cribs," dance halls, and false-front saloons, businesses on the "Row" operated twenty-four hours a day, providing entertainment to the many free-spending miners. Photo by H. S. Poley, between 1893 and 1896.**
Denver Public Library

ABOVE: The exterior of the Rio Grande Saloon on Xenia
Street in Cripple Creek, Colorado, advertises "Lunches,"
"Muenchner & Imperial Beer," and "Union Lager Beer"
to entice the many men of the camp to "Come On In!"
Photo by Nils T. Schedin, circa 1899-1901.
Denver Public Library

ABOVE: Interior view of a Meeker, Colorado, saloon, complete with hand and foot rails, back bar mirror, typical advertising, spittoons, and mustache towels, c. July 5, 1899.
Colorado Historical Society/Denver Public Library

ABOVE: Several men pose outside the Arcade Saloon in Eldora, Colorado, about 1898. Once a popular mining camp, Eldora is now a ghost town located in the midst of ski country. Photo by Martin R. Parsons.
Colorado Historical Society/Denver Public Library

ABOVE: **The bartender stands behind the bar in the White Dog Saloon in Sanborn, Colorado, circa 1898. One patron waves a gun in one hand and a cigar in the other as two more customers look on.**
Denver Public Library

A GRASSY RESORT,

LEFT: **Called the "Grassy Resort," this saloon in Grassy, Colorado, hosts a group of working men warming up next to a wood-fired stove. Photo by H. S. Poley, circa 1895.** *Denver Public Library*

ABOVE: **Miners pose before a makeshift tent saloon in the mining camp of Creede, the last silver boomtown in Colorado, about 1892. Mining continued in the area for nearly 100 years.** *Colorado Historical Society/Denver Public Library*

190. THE BAR. THE COLORADO, GLENWOOD

ABOVE: **Two bartenders await their customers behind the bar of the Hotel Colorado in Glenwood Springs, Colorado. No expense was spared in building the opulent hotel, called the "Grande Dame," in 1893. Today, visitors to the historic hotel continue to enjoy the same service and magnificence as did those of more than a century ago.**
Denver Public Library

ABOVE: **Situated in the "red light district" of Cripple Creek, Colorado, was Crapper Jack's Saloon. The photograph, made between 1895 and 1899, shows both men and women with drinks in hand making a toast. Due to its location on Myers Avenue, these women were most likely "painted ladies," there for the enjoyment of the male patrons.**
Denver Public Library

LEFT: **The Fountain Saloon in Cripple Creek, Colorado, was visited by both the working class man and the rich. Here on the corner of 4th Street and Myers Avenue, customers pose with co-owner Marus Durand before the double door entry to the saloon, circa 1896-1900.**
Denver Public Library

ABOVE: **Bartender Gus Kitzman looks over the crowd in Louie Wolfe's saloon in Silver Cliff, Colorado, circa 1895-1905. Should the customers need a cigar or a pinch of tobacco, the saloon makes both available in the display cases next to the bar.**
Denver Public Library

FAR LEFT: Andren Sylvester, complete with beret and mustache, stands behind the bar at his small saloon in Georgetown, Colorado, circa 1892-1900. Behind him, liquor bottles line the shelves against beadboard and Victorian wallpaper.
Denver Public Library

LEFT: The Holy Moses Saloon, named after the nearby Holy Moses Mine, some 2.5 miles northeast of Creede, Colorado, stands next to the rocky canyon walls that surround the town, circa 1890. Owner Mr. William Orthen, in shirtsleeves, was quick to welcome the many miners as they ended their day in the dark mines and headed for relief inside his saloon. Later, Orthen would become the sheriff of Creede.
Denver Public Library

ABOVE: **Patrons lean against the handrail of the Weaver Brothers Saloon in Breckenridge, Colorado. Typical saloon décor includes chintz wallpaper, cigar advertisements, and large back bar mirror. In this 1890-1900 photograph, obviously before the times of strict health codes, a black Labrador Retriever lounges atop the polished bar.** *Denver Public Library*

ABOVE: **J. P. Anderson's Scandinavian House,**
located at 1719 Blake Street in downtown
Denver, Colorado, was a popular stopping
place for city dwellers. Here, in about 1890,
the bartender and patrons pose for the
camera before the well-patronized saloon,
adorned with Coors advertising.
Denver Public Library

ABOVE: Faro was the game of choice for most gamblers in the Old West, including these men in a Morenci, Arizona, saloon in about 1895. Today, Faro is an almost forgotten game, as modern casinos do not offer it because odds to the house are not favorable enough.
Peter Newark's American Pictures

RIGHT: This faro game in Bisbee, Arizona, appears to be a "hot" one as several men gather around the table to watch the action, circa 1903.
Peter Newark's American Pictures

LEFT: **Inside George Laman's Saloon in the copper mining town of Jerome, Arizona, in about 1897. Located high atop Cleopatra Hill at 5,200 feet in elevation, the settlement provided few comforts to its many miners except for its numerous saloons and brothels.**
Peter Newark's American Pictures

ABOVE: **Bartenders pose in one of the few saloons of the historic silver camp of Montezuma, Colorado, circa 1890-1900. Sitting at an elevation of over 10,000 feet, Montezuma is all but a ghost town today.**
Denver Public Library

ABOVE: **Ten men and a boy pose on the board sidewalk outside a saloon in Freeland, Colorado, in the 1890s. Yet another mining camp, not only is the saloon long gone, but the entire town as well.**
Denver Public Library

RIGHT: Gathered around a pot-bellied stove, drinking and smoking, these men stop playing billiards for a moment to pose for a photograph in a Trinidad, Colorado, saloon, seen in the 1890s. A sign near the bar reads "No Minor or Habitual Drunkard" as a stuffed heron looks on.
Denver Public Library

RIGHT: In 1899, Wyatt Earp, along with his partner Charlie Hoxie, established the Second Class Saloon in Nome, Alaska, during the great Gold Rush. Complete with false front and boardwalk porch, the two-story saloon boasted colorful signage portraying it as "The Only Second Class Saloon in Alaska." The saloon, along with the larger part of the business district, burned down in 1906; this photo was made in about 1899.
Peter Newark's American Pictures

FAR RIGHT: Ever popular, gambling was just as important as drinking in many saloons of the West (circa 1900).
Peter Newark's American Pictures

ABOVE: Situated on one of the main roads into the Basin Mining District, Placerville became a supply base and grew rapidly. In 1863 the town had a population of five thousand people as well as the ever-present saloons. Here, several men pose before Charles F. Rowe's Saloon, about 1900. Today, Placerville is a well-preserved ghost town with only about twenty residents. *Idaho State Historical Society.*

ABOVE: When gold was discovered in the Boise Basin in 1862, dozens of mining camps sprang up, including Idaho City, which soon became the largest town in the territory. A beehive of commercial activity, the town earned a quick reputation for bawdiness in its many saloons, where the price of whiskey was cheaper than water. Here at the Corner Saloon, several men pose at the long polished bar. Joe Shanahan stands behind the bar while his son Carol sits atop.
Idaho State Historical Society

ABOVE: An Emmett, Idaho, peace officer stands at the long polished bar of the Russell Hotel Saloon. Enjoying a drink, he props his boot along the brass foot rail as another customer and the bartender also pose for the camera.
Idaho State Historical Society

RIGHT: Ernst Roeber (left), a German/American wrestling champion in the late 1880s, poses in front of his corner saloon in New York City. Much like athletes of today, many successful sports figures of the past invested their winnings into bars and restaurants.
Library of Congress

LEFT: Jim Haly and his squaw pose with another man and a dog in front of Haly's Road House in Fort Yukon, Alaska, between 1900 and 1916.
Library of Congress

ABOVE: **This dusty Nevada street, with its false-front businesses, provides a bite to eat and a barber, but its highlight is its four saloons.**
National Archives

OVERLEAF LEFT: **This Market Street building in St. Louis, Missouri, features two saloons on its ground floor, one of which displays Lemp Beer. Beginning as a family business, Lemp Beer became one of the largest breweries in the nation in the 19th century, only to be entirely destroyed decades later when Prohibition came into force.**
Corbis

OVERLEAF RIGHT: **On Sacramento Street in what is now San Francisco's Noe Hill District, in the Victorian Heart of the city, once stood the unique What Cheer House. Opened in 1852, the hotel catered only to men and served no alcohol. But for thirsty patrons, they needn't have worried, as just two doors down was a liquor store. The What Cheer House burned in the fire of 1906.**
Corbis

ABOVE: **Along the old Spanish Trail, bartenders are ready for their customers to come off the range at the Stockmen's Bar in Saguache, Colorado, circa 1901.**
Denver Public Library

ABOVE: At the end of the 19th century, Turret, Colorado, was one of the many bustling gold camps in Chaffee County. Here, many of the miners gather at a popular saloon bedecked with a deer's head and the traditional long bar and mirror. Today, Turret is one of the many remaining Old West ghost towns to be found in Colorado. *Denver Public Library*

LEFT: **Cigars, whiskey, and beer were served up freely at yet one more of the many Cripple Creek, Colorado, saloons. However, in this photo, made between 1900 and 1907, the patrons don't seem to be actively partaking of the bartenders' wares. Photo by Nils T. Schedin.**
Denver Public Library

ABOVE: **Seven men pose outside Jim Ganson's saloon in Idlewild, Colorado. The log building sports two Schlitz signs at its front corner posts, and there's a steep roof so that the heavy snows will easily melt and slide during the winter. Photo by Art West, circa 1903.**
Denver Public Library

ABOVE: **Customers gather around the bar and raise beer glasses inside a saloon in the mining town of Turret, Chaffee County, Colorado, circa 1903. Note the large portrait of a woman above the back bar mirror, common in the saloons of the West.** *Denver Public Library*

RIGHT: **Weigel's Saloon was originally built as the Miner's Exchange Saloon in 1865. The establishment acquired its original name from the practice of exchanging gold dust for legal tender, or a good drink. In this photo three men play poker as Melvin Weigel looks on from behind the bar.** *Idaho State Historical Society*

LEFT: **This photograph shows Weigel's Saloon as it has been updated to include billiard tables. Today, the historic Miner's Exchange establishment is one of the oldest buildings in the State of Idaho and is now home to Bosie County offices. The original bar and back bar have become the desk for the County Commissioners meetings.**
Idaho State Historical Society

LEFT: **A mining and fishing community, lined with shops and saloons, Wrangell, Alaska, looks in this 1901 photograph to be a dreary place to live, but someone obviously found value in the community as it is one of the oldest in the state. Wyatt Earp served as a temporary marshal for ten days while he and his wife, Josie, were on their way to the Klondike.**
Library of Congress

PREVIOUS PAGES LEFT: "No Loafing Allowed" at Perley McBride's Saloon, circa 1906. Though this bored-looking bartender appears as if he could use some company, the next customer better have the price of a drink if he intends to stay.
Corbis

PREVIOUS PAGES RIGHT: A group of theater performers, including women and a small girl, pose before the camera with full glasses raised in a toast in front of the Brunswick Saloon, between 1900 and 1910. Located at the corner of South Spruce and East Colorado Avenue in Telluride, Colorado, the Brunswick Saloon was near the "red light district."
Denver Public Library

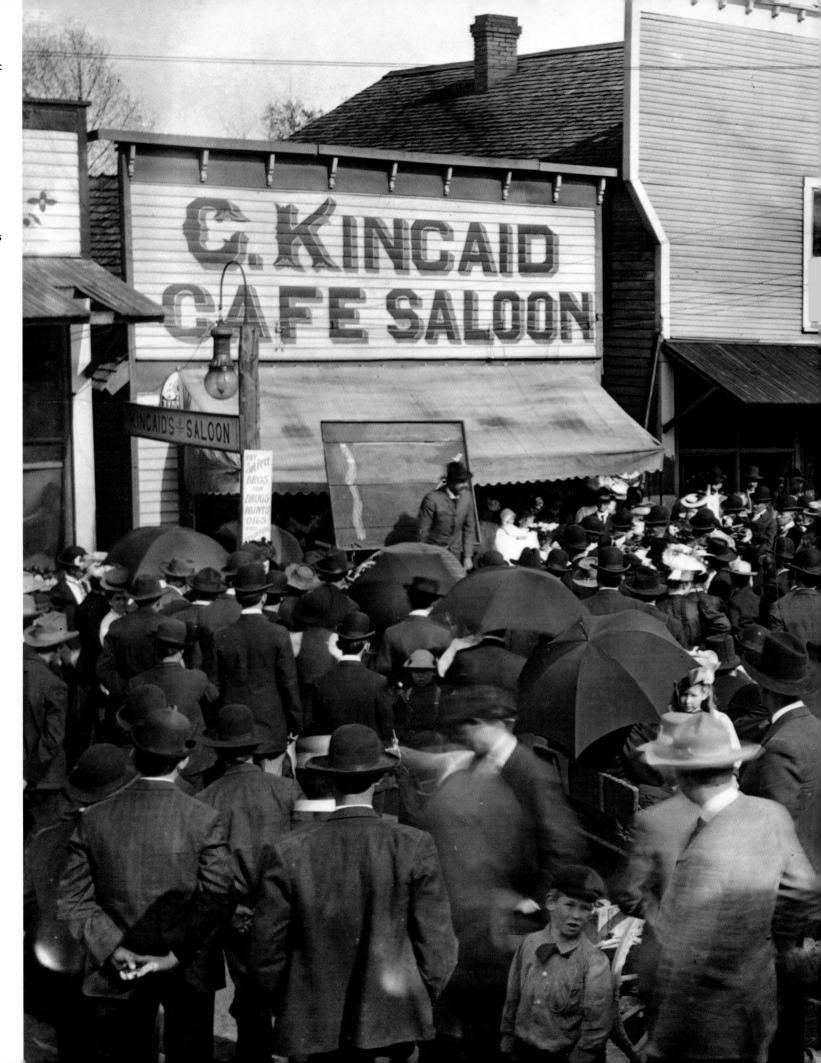

LEFT: Evangelist Farem preaches a sermon directly in front of the C. Kincaid Café Saloon in Corbin, Kentucky, in about 1908, no doubt touting the ills of alcohol consumption. Nonetheless, a large crowd gathers to hear his words, *Corbis*

ABOVE: Several men pose in front of the bar at the Shanahan & Haggert Saloon, Idaho City, in about 1916. Co-proprietor Joe Shanahan is pictured fourth from the right. The man at the far left is the deputy sheriff. *Idaho State Historical Society*

RIGHT: Beginning as a stop along the Oregon Trail, Pocatello grew rapidly when the discovery of gold in 1860 brought a wave of settlers to the region. Pictured here in about 1910 is bartender and owner Al Roulet behind his bar. Note the ever-popular "ladies" hung above the bar. *Idaho State Historical Society*

LEFT: **A thirsty cowpuncher rides his horse through a Colorado saloon, then calmly sips his drink as other men look on, November 1, 1907.** *Library of Congress*

ABOVE: **In 1905, it's a lively day in front of A. J. Rustad's Saloon in Moorhead, Minnesota. Alas, the fate of Rustad's, along with many other Moorhead saloons, was doomed when Moorhead went "dry" just ten years later.** *Clay County Minnesota Historical Society*

OVERLEAF LEFT: **Having fun for the camera, six cowboys and a bartender pretend to shoot guns at the feet of a tenderfoot, or novice, who is made to dance, in an Old West saloon, c. 1907.** *Corbis*

OVERLEAF RIGHT: **Thirsty cowboys from the LS Ranch belly up to the bar in Tascosa, Texas. Once one of the largest ranches in the Texas Panhandle, the 221,000-acre spread at one time employed Pat Garrett, Billy the Kid's killer, as a gunman to control cattle rustling. Photo by Erwin E. Smith, c. 1908.** *Corbis*

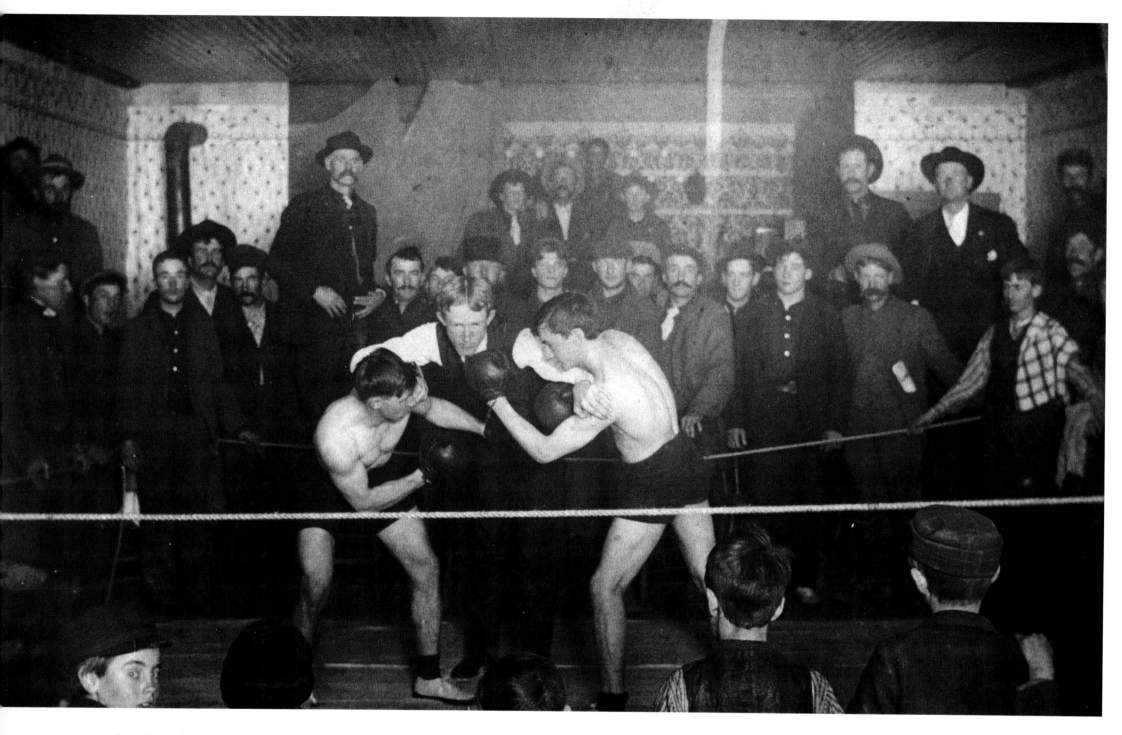

ABOVE: As a form of entertainment for their customers, saloons often held boxing matches to attract the crowds. Such was the case at the Woods Saloon in Turret, Colorado. In addition to enjoying the spectator sport, there was, no doubt, money changing hands as gamblers tried to predict the winners. Photo by Frank L. Hall, circa 1905.
Denver Public Library

RIGHT: Framed pictures of women bedeck the Victorian wallpaper in the Union Saloon at 605 Colorado Avenue in Colorado City, Colorado, in 1910. Advertisements also entice customers with: "Walters Gold Label Beer In Bottles," "Anheuser-Busch," and "Goetz Brewing Co."
Denver Public Library

ABOVE: Before Prohibition, Colorado City offered a "drinker's alternative" to its "dry" neighbor, Colorado Springs, to the east. Numerous saloons along this Colorado City boulevard offered tobacco, billiards, and alcohol to the many who flocked to the smaller town. Alas, it ended for these profitable businesses when Colorado Springs annexed Colorado City in 1917. Photo by Horace S. Poley, circa 1900-1913. *Denver Public Library*

RIGHT: Al Anderson bartends at Hank Trimble's Saloon in Lewiston, Idaho. Trimble was a successful miner who took hundreds of thousands of dollars of ore from the ground in Idaho and Montana before establishing this saloon. Later he became a large rancher and landowner. *Idaho State Historical Society*

OVERLEAF LEFT: Two young boys hawk newspapers in front of a popular St. Louis, Missouri, saloon, circa May, 1910. The Anti-Saloon League and other temperance groups would have been concerned that such youngsters, who also included little girls, worked so close to saloons and bars, selling to the patrons. *Library of Congress*

OVERLEAF RIGHT: A saloon adjoins the Johnston Branch of the St. Louis Post Dispatch at 10th and Cass Streets, May 1910. Painted signs on the wall of the saloon shout "Alpen Briesu," draft and bottled beer, and 10¢ whiskä, while young boys gather beneath, hoping to sell newspapers to the patrons. *Library of Congress*

ABOVE: **At the Louvre in Reno, Nevada, men enjoy drinks at the bar while open gambling is on offer, in 1910. Ironically, Nevada would ban casinos the same year, only to legalize them once again in 1927.**
Library of Congress

RIGHT: **Frank Carpenter and another man stand with their horses in front of a mountain roadhouse, the kind of restaurant/rooming establishment that would have provided meals and drinks to travelers, between 1900 and 1916.**
Library of Congress

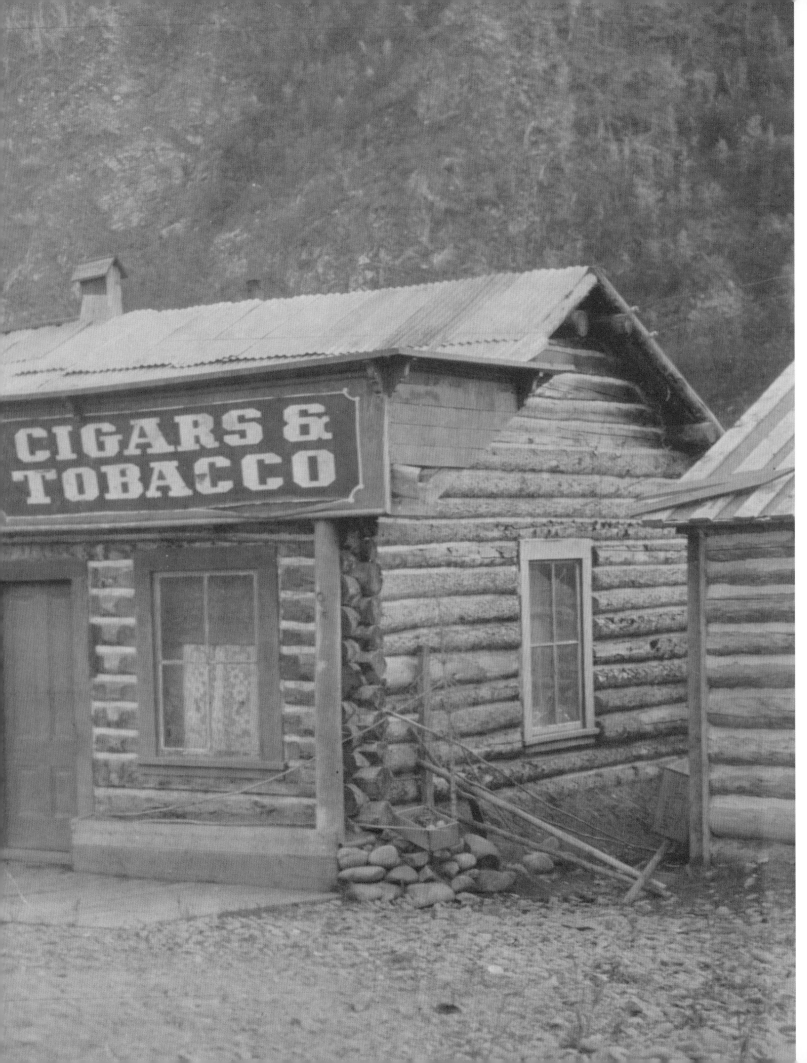

RIGHT: **A group of men "carry on" playfully on the steps of a Chicopee Falls, Massachusetts, saloon. Photo by Lewis W. Hine, June 29, 1916.**
Library of Congress

IGLOO
INN.

BARTHEL'S
DRAUGHT
BEER
MARQUETTE
RYE

ABOVE: Between 1900 and 1916, men gather at the door of the Igloo Inn in Fairbanks, Alaska, a few miles south of the Klondike gold mining area, which brought thousands of gold-seeking customers to the region, intent on finding supplies and rest and relaxation in the saloons that sprang up there
Library of Congress

RIGHT: Gambling in saloons was as much a part of these many establishments as the long polished bar. Here, several men make their wagers as more look on, including the bartender. Note a sign of the times (c.1913)—every single man has facial hair. *Bettmann/Corbis*

LEFT: Duck hunting is and always has been a popular sport in Missouri. Here, two proud men display the fruits of their hunting efforts in a Missouri saloon in 1913.
Corbis

ABOVE: Townspeople watch as World War I army soldiers march through the streets of Brownsville, Texas, past the saloons that entice them. Photo by George Grantham Bain, c.1916,
Corbis

OVERLEAF: Surrounded by the typical trappings of turn of the early 20th century saloons, several bartenders patiently await the drinking crowd in Essex, Connecticut. Photo by Hauser, circa 1910.
Corbis

LEFT: **A classic example of art imitating life, this photo of the Cosmopolitan Saloon in Telluride, Colorado, looks as if it came straight out of an Old West film. Complete with roulette/faro table, vested bartender,** and even Marshal Kenneth Maclean at the end of the long polished bar, it's missing only the piano player and the dancehall girls. Photo by Joseph E. Byers, c.1905-1915. *Corbis*

ABOVE: **The Subway Tavern at 27 Bleeker Street, in the Greenwich Village district of New York City, entices customers with everything from Pilsener beers, to cigars, to ice cream and soda, circa 1905.** *Corbis*

ABOVE: Two customers lounge against a carved wooden bar in Denver, Colorado. A mustached bartender stands before a back bar mirror, cash register, and multiple saloon-type advertising, between 1910 and 1915.
William W. Cecil Collection, Colorado Historical Society/Denver Public Library

ABOVE RIGHT: **View of the interior of a saloon in the Brown Palace Hotel in Denver, Colorado, about 1911. Opened in 1892, the Brown Palace Hotel has never closed, not even for a day, though it has undergone** numerous renovations throughout the years. Even in its earliest days, the Brown Palace exuded opulence, which can be seen in the marble bar, mirrors, and light fixtures. *Denver Public Library*

OVERLEAF LEFT: **A bartender smokes a cigar behind the bar in a saloon associated with the Rocky Mountain Fuel Company, as patrons sit nearby, circa 1910-1920. The Rocky Mountain Fuel Company was unique** among Colorado Coal operations, as it was run by a woman who fought to improve conditions for miners and believed in treating her employees very well.
Denver Public Library

OVERLEAF RIGHT: **Inside a Denver, Colorado, saloon, men pose at the carved wooden bar with pennants hanging above advertising Tivoli Beer and M & O Cigars, circa 1910-1915.**
Colorado Historical Society/Denver Public Library

ABOVE: **Men pose in front of a saloon owned by Abraham J. R. Cort at 1197 West Alameda Avenue in Denver, Colorado. Signs in the windows read: "Lunch Chile" and "Near Beer On Draught 5¢." Most likely, the photo was taken after enactment of Prohibition—hence the "Near Beer." Photo by Charles S. Lillybridge, c. 1910-1920.**
Colorado Historical Society/Denver Public Library

RIGHT: **Bartenders wait for customers at the Royal Bar, probably located in Seattle, Washington, in 1919. Though the 18th Amendment had already been passed, this opulent saloon and restaurant doesn't seem to care. It wouldn't be until the following year that the Volstead Act was passed to enforce Prohibition laws.**
Museum of History and Industry/Corbis

RIGHT: **Four men stand in front of Jackson's Bar at the "Days of '59" Festival in Idaho Springs, Colorado, which was established by prospectors in the early days of the Colorado Gold Rush, an event that continued to be celebrated in the 1920s. The saloon is named for Indian trader, George Jackson, who first discovered gold in the area.**
Denver Public Library

FAR RIGHT: **From regular folks to businessmen, this Nampa, Idaho, bar thumbs its nose at Prohibition laws as a large crowd happily drinks and plays cards, circa 1926.**
Idaho State Historical Society

ABOVE: Prohibition officers raid a lunch room at 922 Pennsylvania Avenue in Washington, D.C., probably April 25, 1923.
Library of Congress

RIGHT: At the Overland Park Auto Camp in Denver, Colorado, alcoholic beverages appear to be absent as groups of people sip sodas during Prohibition. However, tobacco is still sold in the display cases (circa 1920-1931).
Denver Public Library

LEFT: Adorned in nice suits and straw boater hats, four men enjoy a last drink together before Prohibition begins, c.1919.
Bettman/Corbis

RIGHT: Two Prohibition officers pose with an illegal still they have confiscated, circa 1921-1933. Dare they taste the produce, especially while on duty? How else are they to determine that the somewhat murky beverage is actually outlawed liquor?
Library of Congress

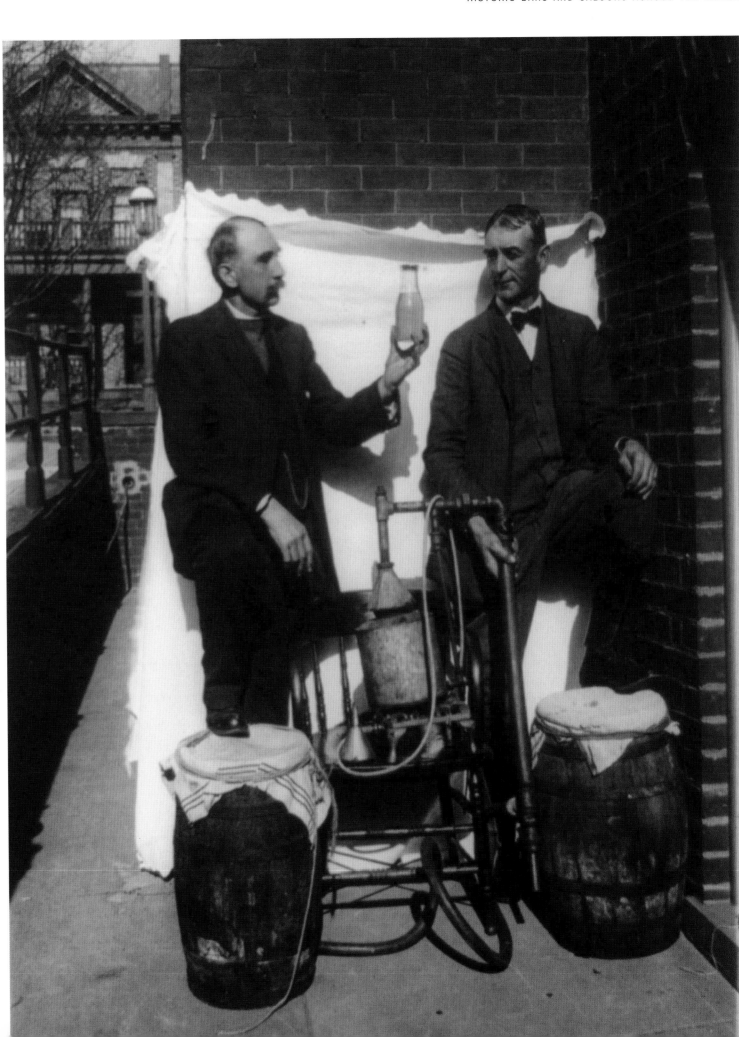

ABOVE: **On a cold and dreary day in January, bootleggers imagine wearing stripes as they are loaded into a paddy wagon in Washington, D.C. The culprits were caught by Capitol police after a thrilling chase through some of the busiest streets of the city, January 21, 1922.**
Library of Congress

LEFT: **A revenue agent poses wearing a "Whiskey Waistcoat," designed to hide bootlegged liquor during the Prohibition era, January 1, 1923.**
Hulton Collection/Getty Images

LEFT: **A pair of "bootlegs" found in the office of Lincoln C. Andrews, Assistant Treasury Department Secretary in charge of Customs, Coast Guard, and Prohibition. Miss Hattie Klawans, a clerk in the office of the "Prohibition Czar," poses with her new Russian boots, often used by women to hide their flasks (circa 1920-1932).**
Library of Congress

LEFT: **During Prohibition, flasks became widely popular among men and women alike. Pictured here is Mlle Rhea, a dancer, demonstrating hiding a flask in her garter, January 26, 1926.**
Library of Congress

LEFT: Two fascinated young boys look on as a police officer stands alongside a wrecked car and cases of bootlegged liquor, November 16, 1922.
Library of Congress

RIGHT: J. M. McCall, proprietor of the Malamute Saloon in Los Angeles, celebrates his grand re-opening by holding a liquor bottle high in the air, c.1932. During Prohibition, the business survived as a restaurant but, suspecting it to be a speakeasy, authorities raided it, only to find nothing but soft drinks and sandwiches. Note the sign that now welcomes women into the establishment.
Corbis

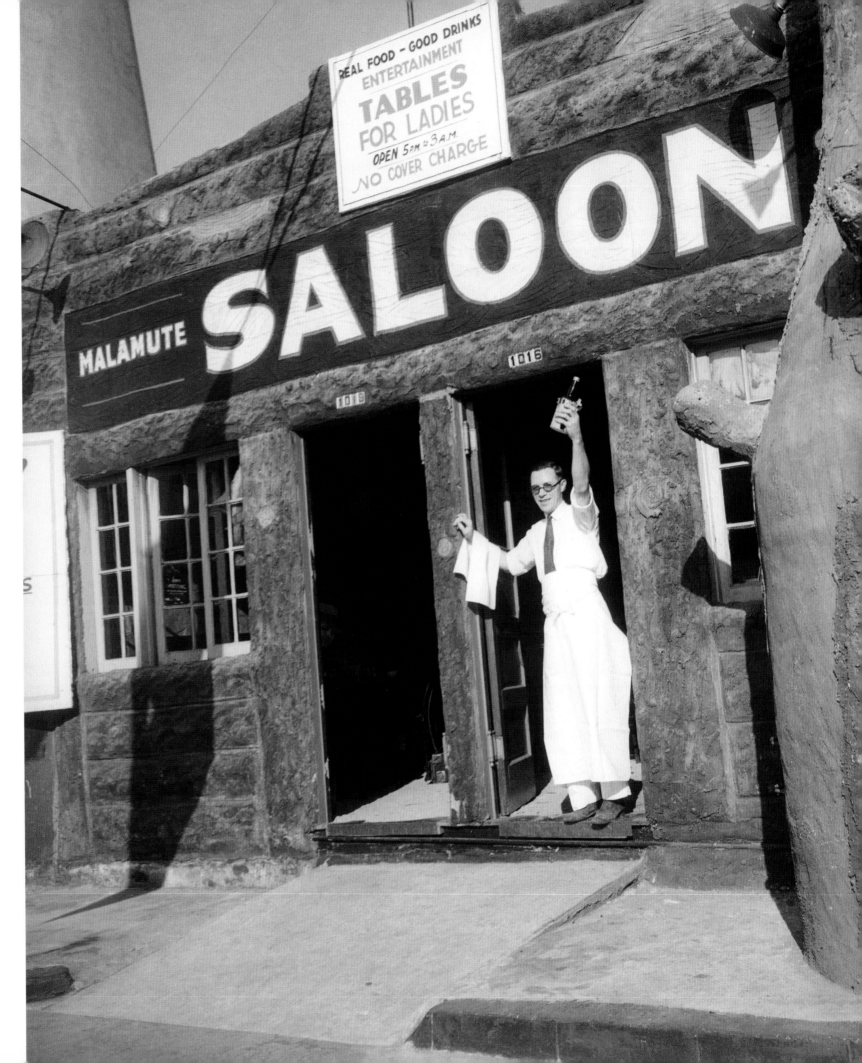

ABOVE: Though one would think these three law enforcement officers would be happy to have made a successful raid on bootleggers in Natrona County, Wyoming, they look anything but. The photo, taken May 8, 1925, displays eight dismantled whiskey stills, along with copper tubing and two rifles leaning up against the stills.
Denver Public Library

ABOVE: Men and women alike enjoy cocktails at the Hunt Club, a popular speakeasy in New York City. To protect themselves from a Prohibition raid, the Hunt Club utilized a filing system that listed their 23,000 eligible customers. Each and every time an unknown customer entered through their doors, the list was checked to ensure eligibility. Photo by Margaret Bourke-White, circa 1933.
Time & Life Pictures/Getty Images

OVERLEAF: Broad smiles and a toast accompany a round of drinks on the house poured by bartenders at Sloppy Joe's Bar in Chicago, Illinois, May 12, 1933. After thirteen years, these happy customers and bar staff are celebrating the announcement of the repeal of the 18th Amendment.
Hulton Collection/American Stock/Getty Images